T0157188

The Infinity Bible

A Family Book of Life

R. B.

Order this book online at www.trafford.com
or email orders@trafford.com

Most Trafford titles are also available at major online book retailers.

Printed in the United States of America.

ISBN: 978-1-4669-7680-1 (sc)
ISBN: 978-1-4669-7681-8 (e)

Trafford rev. 02/28/2013

 www.trafford.com

North America & international
toll-free: 1 888 232 4444 (USA & Canada)
phone: 250 383 6864 ♦ fax: 812 355 4082

My Soul Belongs To Jesus Christ

_____

Please print

10 Ways To Life From The Tree Of Life

His Family (Last Name)	Her Family (Last Name)

1. _____   1. _____

2. _____   2. _____

3. _____   3. _____

4. _____   4. _____

5. _____   5. _____

Memo's To Jesus

I.

Thou shalt not have
no other Gods
before me.

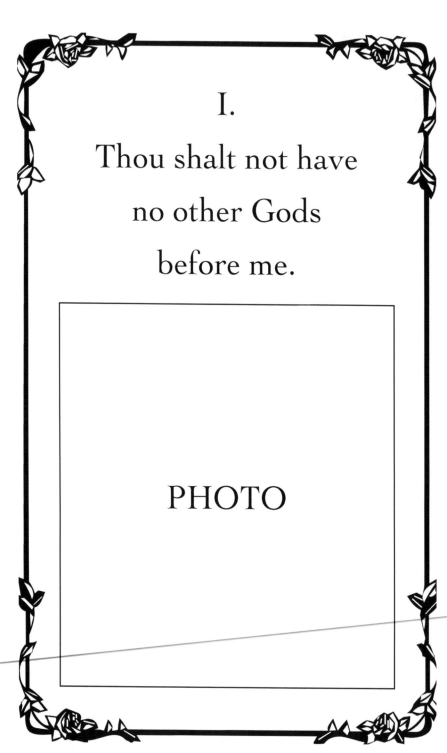

PHOTO

1. Name _____

2. Relationship to Me _____

3. Date of Birth _____

4. Occupation _____

5. Testimonies of Life _____

_____

_____

_____

_____

_____

6. Repent for the Lord for which; He is good. _____

_____

_____

_____

_____

_____

7. Date of Rebirth. _____

_____

_____

_____

_____

_____

_____

8. Days of Blessing in the Name of the Lord. _____

_____

_____

_____

_____

_____

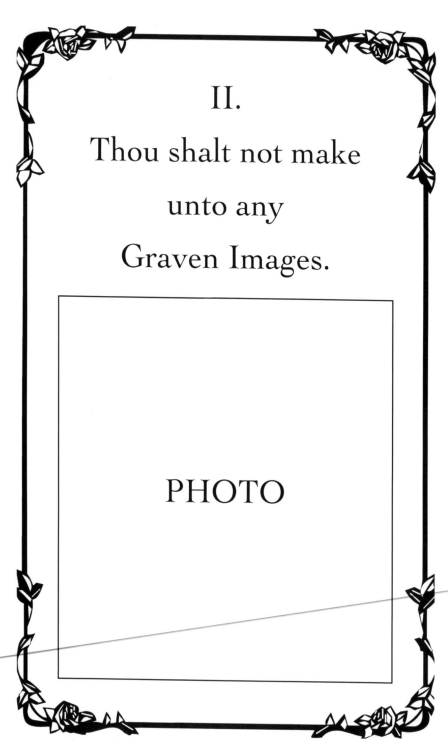

II.

Thou shalt not make

unto any

Graven Images.

PHOTO

1. Name _____

2. Relationship to Me _____

3. Date of Birth _____

4. Occupation _____

5. Testimonies of Life _____

_____

_____

_____

_____

_____

6. Repent for the Lord for which; He is good. _____

_____

_____

_____

_____

_____

7. Date of Rebirth. _____

_____

_____

_____

_____

_____

8. Days of Blessing in the Name of the Lord. _____

_____

_____

_____

_____

_____

_____

III.

Thou shalt not take the name of the Lord thy God in Vain.

PHOTO

1. Name _____

2. Relationship to Me _____

3. Date of Birth _____

4. Occupation _____

5. Testimonies of Life _____

_____

_____

_____

_____

_____

_____

6. Repent for the Lord for which; He is good. _____

_____

_____

_____

_____

_____

_____

7. Date of Rebirth. _____

_____

_____

_____

_____

_____

_____

8. Days of Blessing in the Name of the Lord. _____

_____

_____

_____

_____

_____

IV.

Remember the Sabbath Day to keep it Holy.

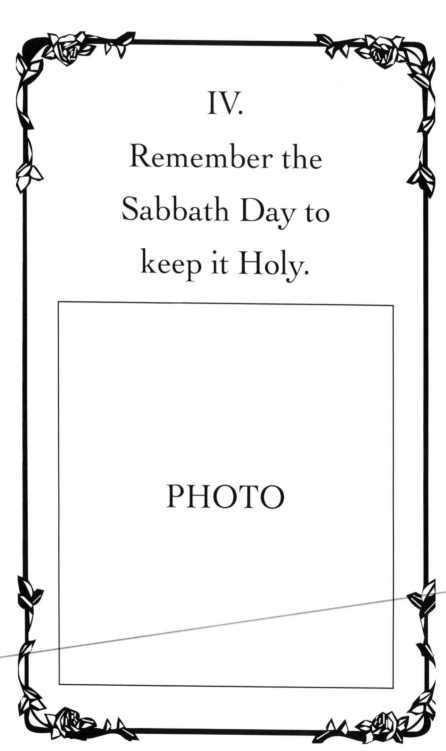

PHOTO

1. Name _____

2. Relationship to Me _____

3. Date of Birth _____

4. Occupation _____

5. Testimonies of Life _____

_____

_____

_____

_____

_____

_____

6. Repent for the Lord for which; He is good. _____

_____

_____

_____

_____

_____

7. Date of Rebirth. _____

_____

_____

_____

_____

_____

_____

8. Days of Blessing in the Name of the Lord. _____

_____

_____

_____

_____

_____

_____

V.

Honor thy Father and thy Mother.

PHOTO

1. Name _____

2. Relationship to Me _____

3. Date of Birth _____

4. Occupation _____

5. Testimonies of Life _____

_____

_____

_____

_____

_____

_____

6. Repent for the Lord for which; He is good. _____

_____

_____

_____

_____

_____

_____

7. Date of Rebirth. _____

_____

_____

_____

_____

_____

_____

8. Days of Blessing in the Name of the Lord. _____

_____

_____

_____

_____

_____

VI.
Thou Shalt not Kill.

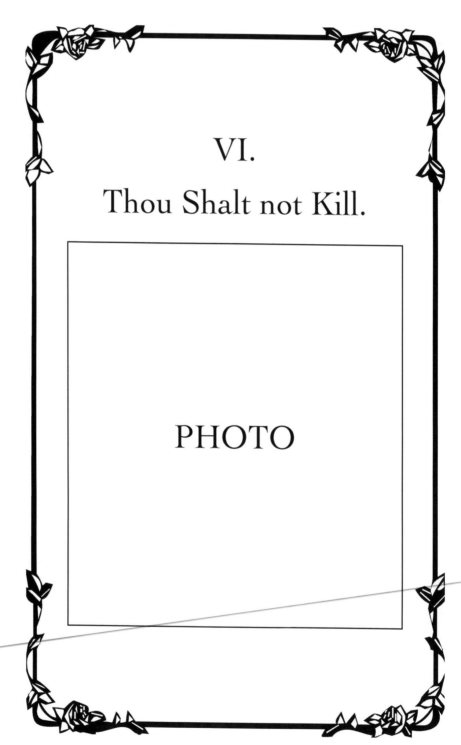

PHOTO

1. Name _____

2. Relationship to Me _____

3. Date of Birth _____

4. Occupation _____

5. Testimonies of Life _____

_____

_____

_____

_____

_____

6. Repent for the Lord for which; He is good. _____

_____

_____

_____

_____

_____

7. Date of Rebirth. _____

_____

_____

_____

_____

_____

8. Days of Blessing in the Name of the Lord. _____

_____

_____

_____

_____

_____

VII.

Thou shalt
not commit Adultery.

PHOTO

1. Name _____

2. Relationship to Me _____

3. Date of Birth _____

4. Occupation _____

5. Testimonies of Life _____

   _____

   _____

   _____

   _____

   _____

6. Repent for the Lord for which; He is good. _____

_____

_____

_____

_____

_____

7. Date of Rebirth. _____

_____

_____

_____

_____

_____

8. Days of Blessing in the Name of the Lord. _____

_____

_____

_____

_____

_____

_____

VIII.

Thou shalt not steal.

PHOTO

1. Name _____

2. Relationship to Me _____

3. Date of Birth _____

4. Occupation _____

5. Testimonies of Life _____

_____

_____

_____

_____

_____

_____

6. Repent for the Lord for which; He is good. _____

_____

_____

_____

_____

_____

7. Date of Rebirth. _____

_____

_____

_____

_____

_____

8. Days of Blessing in the Name of the Lord. _____

_____

_____

_____

_____

_____

_____

IX.

Thou shalt not bear False Witness against thy Neighbor.

PHOTO

1. Name _____

2. Relationship to Me _____

3. Date of Birth _____

4. Occupation _____

5. Testimonies of Life _____

_____

_____

_____

_____

_____

_____

6. Repent for the Lord for which; He is good. _____

_____

_____

_____

_____

_____

7. Date of Rebirth. _____

_____

_____

_____

_____

_____

8. Days of Blessing in the Name of the Lord. _____

_____

_____

_____

_____

_____

_____

X.

Thou shalt not Covet.

PHOTO

1. Name _____

2. Relationship to Me _____

3. Date of Birth _____

4. Occupation _____

5. Testimonies of Life _____

_____

_____

_____

_____

_____

_____

6. Repent for the Lord for which; He is good. _____

_____

_____

_____

_____

_____

7. Date of Rebirth. _____

_____

_____

_____

_____

_____

8. Days of Blessing in the Name of the Lord. _____

_____

_____

_____

_____

_____

_____

He always had a nature of God.

Instead of This, of his own Free will he gave up all;
   he had.

He became like a human likeness.

He was humble and walked the obedience all the way
   to death—his death on the Cross.

And so, In honor of the name of Jesus all beings in
   heaven, on earth, and in the world below.

And all will openly proclaim that Jesus Christ is Lord.

To the glory of God the Father.

Printed in the United States
By Bookmasters